'We use poetry when we want to speak our souls or our hearts,
both as writers and readers ...'

Carol Ann Duffy, The Times, *October 2011*

WORDSMITH

The Gift of a Soul

Megan Young & Merrilyn Thomas

M MEDLAR TREE PUBLISHING

First published in July 2013 by Medlar Tree Publishing,
9 Church Road, Oare, Faversham, Kent ME13 0QA
www.wordsmiththebook.com
wordsmiththebook@gmail.com

This edition published in January 2014

Designed by Sue Pressley, Stonecastle Graphics
Sutton Valence, Kent ME17 3HZ

Printed and bound by Headley Brothers Ltd, The Invicta Press,
Queen's Road, Ashford, Kent TN24 8HH

This publication has been facilitated by the Cancer of Unknown
Primary (CUP) Foundation – Jo's Friends. (www.cupfoundjo.org)
A donation will be made to the CUP Foundation from the sale
of each copy of this book.

ACKNOWLEDGEMENTS

I would like to thank Megan's husband, Toby Broad, for entrusting me with Megan's poetry and for all the help he has given me. I have chosen to refer to Megan by her maiden name as she was known as Megan Young professionally and wrote much of the poetry in this book under that name. However, she was extremely proud of being Mrs Broad, a fact which should not go unacknowledged. My thanks also go to my daughter Morag for the wise and perceptive advice she has given me during the course of compiling this volume. I have treasured her support during a difficult time for us both.

I am enormously grateful to my dear friend Gill Bailey who has guided me through the process of producing this book. She has shared with me the professional expertise she has acquired during her long career as a publisher and her advice has been invaluable. My thanks also go to John Symons, the founder and director of The Cancer of Unknown Primary (CUP) Foundation – Jo's Friends. It has been a privilege to work with him and I am grateful for the sensitive manner in which he has helped me.

Thank you also to Gillian McClure, Catherine Bennet-Williams and Beth Patel for telling me about the Megan they knew; Elisabeth Calvert for a stroke of genius; Alan Hamilton for his vital assistance; Liz Britton for practical help and more; and Sue Pressley for her empathetic design and way in which she came to know Megan through her poetry.

There are many people – both friends and family – who have helped me over the past four years, some in ways that are not directly linked to the publication of this book. To you all I say thank you for your loving support. In particular I would like to mention Martin Turner and the late Amanda Evans who helped me in my need to better understand what Megan already knew.

Merrilyn Thomas

To The Reader

This is a gift of my soul.
All that I have, all that I am is here.
I am a scientist, an artist, a Wordsmith.
This is the blood of the Wordsmith, it is pain.
Understand me, Love me and if not,
at least Believe me.

Megan Frances Young, circa 1998

These words were written by Megan on the first page of the dilapidated old file in which she kept her poetry. I did not see them until after her death and nor, I believe, did anyone else. This is her introduction to her poetry, to her life.

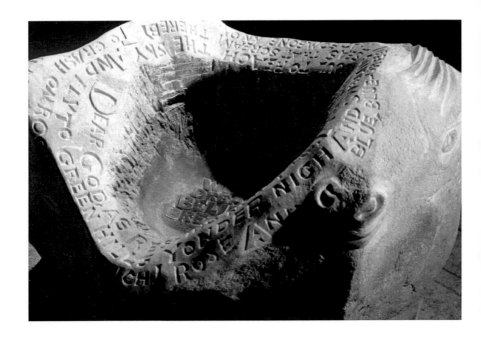

Megan's Rock, sculpted from Preseli Mountain bluestone by the Pembrokeshire sculptor Darren Yeadon. Megan's poem, For A Seagull, *is engraved around the Rock.*

FOR A SEAGULL

Dear God, as resting now I lie,
I pray my soul to reach the sky
To fly to green hills yonder nigh,
And swelling seas that scream thereby
To crash on rocks from which I rose
And blue, blue-green that someone knows,
Dear God, that in my time of rest
My spirit wanders to the West.
And if I die before I wake,
My country, then, my soul shall take.

March 1994

My daughter Megan died from an unknown form of cancer on 18 January 2010 at the age of 32. Megan was an equine veterinary surgeon, a poet, a musician, a wife, a mother, and a passionate horsewoman. She was gifted, headstrong, compassionate, tempestuous, beautiful and wise.

She was born in Greenwich Hospital, London on 28 July 1977 at about 5.30pm. It had been a bright sunny day. Megan was our first child. This was shortly before the days when a simple scan would reveal the sex of your child but it was no surprise to me that our baby was a girl. Throughout my pregnancy, I had been certain that the child within me would be a little girl with brown eyes. I could imagine no other. I felt very close to my baby long before she was born.

Megan was conceived in St David's, Pembrokeshire one day in October 1976. I don't know if I ever told her this. Probably not. Too much information, people would say. Whether I did or not, Megan was imbued with the spirit of Pembrokeshire throughout her life, probably from that day. The earth, rocks and sea from which many generations of her ancestors had sprung, were for her tangible, real, alive.

One day, when Megan was around three or four weeks old, I was sitting in my nursing chair, holding her to the breast. I looked down at this helpless tiny infant, so precious to me, so dependent, so very much loved, and I thought to myself that one day this child would bring me unimaginable grief. I was aware, at that moment, that this was a strange thought. Should I not be musing on the happiness she would bring to me? But the thought was unbidden and very strong; so strong that it has always remained with me. My rational mind told me that it was the awareness of my love for my baby which caused this thought to enter my mind, the knowledge that it is only great love which can cause such sorrow. Perhaps, I now wonder, perhaps there was another, less rational reason, a real sensing of things to come.

Megan started writing poetry almost as soon as she could form the letters. When she was sixteen she wrote a poem which encapsulated in a few lines not only her love of Pembrokeshire, particularly the rugged coast between St David's and Fishguard where generations of her family had farmed the land, but also her spiritual awareness. Of all the many poems that she wrote during her brief life, this one ranks as one of the most significant. It lived with her. She returned to it on many occasions, tweaking it here and there, and in 2001, having just completed her final veterinary examinations, she read it at her Welsh grandfather's funeral.

This simple poem is now engraved around a large slab of bluestone rock from Pembrokeshire's Preseli Mountains, the same rock as that which was transported so many centuries ago to form the stone circle at Stonehenge. This ancient rock, millions of years old, has been carved by Darren Yeadon, a Pembrokeshire sculptor, not as a memorial but as an eternal tribute to a remarkable young woman. The Rock now stands beside a field on the farm in Kent from which Megan ran her veterinary practice.

This book is also a tribute to Megan but it is one she has created herself. I am simply the means of its production. The day she died, a beautiful bright and sunny winter's day, as she lay on her bed at home, I told her that I would publish her poetry. Although at this stage she could not speak, she was able to communicate with her eyes. On hearing my words, her face lit up with joy.

This is my promise to her.

Megan was diagnosed with cancer in September 2009. She was a supremely fit and healthy young woman. All who knew her were stunned by the news. But many also felt sure she would come through it. If anyone can beat it, Megan will, they said. But Megan knew that her survival would be a miracle. As a vet, she was aware of the medical significance of the form of cancerous cell which was invading her body. It was rare and aggressive, a form known as mucinous adenocarcinoma which meant that the disease had spread throughout her abdomen like a thin curtain of cancerous cells.

Lying in her hospital bed, she often tried to explain to me the medical science of her condition, patiently and concisely describing what was going on in her body as though giving a seminar to a rather dim first year medical student. Her body was riddled with secondary cancers but her doctors were unable to discover the site of the primary tumour. This complicated any treatment for not only could the primary tumour not be surgically removed (since it could not be found), it also meant that chemotherapy was unlikely to be successful as the normal practice is to target the drugs at the site of the cancer from which the patient is suffering. Since the site of the cancer was unknown, targeting was a hit and miss affair. During the course of Megan's illness we were variously told that she might be suffering from ovarian cancer or pancreatic cancer and she was treated with chemotherapy accordingly. However, a post-mortem showed that neither of these diagnoses was correct. But the pathologist was also unable to say with certainty what type of cancer Megan had been suffering from, only what she did not have.

Megan died four months after cancer was diagnosed. It was only after Megan's death, a few weeks after, that I learned from a BBC radio programme that there is a type of cancer known as Cancer of Unknown Primary (CUP) and that many thousands of people fall into this category every year. It is a type of cancer which has fallen below the radar of public knowledge. The nightmare of a cancer diagnosis is compounded by the fact that doctors cannot tell you what type of cancer you are suffering from.

'Cancer of unknown primary is the "orphan" of the cancer world. Most people have never heard of CUP and find it hard to believe that in this scientific age the cause of the cancer spread can remain unknown. But each year in the UK over 10,000 people are diagnosed with CUP. It is the sixth most common cancer for women and the eighth most common for men. Sadly, it is responsible for about the same number of deaths as prostate cancer and almost as many as breast cancer.'

These are the words of a cancer charity founded following the death of Jo Symons from cancer of unknown primary a few days after her 46th birthday. The mission of The Cancer of Unknown Primary (CUP) Foundation, otherwise known as Jo's Friends, is to 'make the unknown, known' by providing information and support to CUP patients and their carers; raising awareness of CUP; and promoting research that improves diagnosis and treatment leading to the end of CUP.

Although Megan knew she was dying, and calmly told us that it was so, she also held out hope, as nearly all human beings do, that something might save her. I do not believe that she thought her saviour would be medical science. She expressed something of these thoughts in a poem she wrote about one month after diagnosis when doctors were still searching for the primary tumour.

LIVE AND LET LIVE

(in which Megan speaks to her tumour)

As I am one of God's children, you must also be.
You find your niche according to His law, somewhere in me.
And, as Darwin predicted, you will struggle and strive
And I shall endeavour to keep us both alive.

I don't suggest it's your fault, though neither is it mine,
That some mutation of your code made you thus malign.
But, given that you are my flesh, my blood, my own,
Not so very different from my precious baby son,

Supposing that you crept, spider-like, back into your hole.
I should not wish you harm for harm's sake,
I'd let you live, I'd coexist with you, each in our quiet way.
No need for enmity or spite. It's not a war.

October 2009 (after diagnosis)

Megan's final poem was written about two months before she died during a brief period when there seemed to have been some improvement in her condition. We – her family – felt an optimism that we hardly dared to acknowledge. Could it be that the miracle would happen? Megan remained realistic. She was dying, she told us. But she was not ready yet. She insisted that I take her Christmas shopping. We went to one of those bleak out-of-town shopping centres where she commandeered a wheelchair and raced around the shops in a manner which saw me crying out in exasperation that she should slow down. I was running to keep up with her, as I had done throughout her life. She bought photograph albums for her husband Toby's present and later filled them with pictures of their life together. A conscious and deliberate gift of a memory.

When Megan and Toby were married in 2004, I did not give them a wedding present as such but said I would do so later when the dust of their great day had settled. About a year later, Megan asked me if I would buy her a horse. She already owned several horses and ponies, chief among them being Lochan, her thoroughbred eventer, and Mac, her wild and woolly Exmoor. The horse she wanted me to buy was another special case – a young Cleveland Bay filly. The Cleveland Bay is England's oldest breed of horse. They are large strong animals. During the 20th century, the breed nearly died out in large part due to losses on the battlefields of the First World War and the decline of the use of horses in agriculture. As a breed, they have been rescued by a few devoted horse enthusiasts, one of them being the Queen. They are used to pull carriages in royal parades. Megan's plan was that in due course she too would breed from her Cleveland Bay filly, which I duly bought and which Megan named Ochre for her beautiful colour. Cleveland Bays are renowned for their docile temperament. They may be large and strong but they are soft and gentle by nature. I am not a natural horse person and, of all Megan's horses, her Cleveland Bay was the only one with which I felt entirely safe. The following poem, Megan's last, is a homage to Ochre.

Megan and Ochre, 2008

THE ROOF OF THE WORLD

The view from the saddle I know very well.
It's about eye level with the stable gutters;
Can inspect the moss and dead leaves as they head for the drainpipe,
Can see into blackbirds' nests in the middle of untrimmed hedges.
Different horses, a little higher or lower perhaps
But never all that far off the ground.

Except for one. My big, big horse.
The usual jokes about oxygen masks, snow on my hat,
Carry a parachute in case you fall off.
And yet it is quieter up here.
Can't hear people wanting, needing, shouting, muttering.
The world looks the same but she's so big it feels smaller.

Everything happens slowly on this saddle.

Sun wanders across the sky,

Time struggles to march through treacle, gives up, meanders.

Birds flap less and glide more.

I own these minutes when I have nowhere else I need to be.

I'm the same rider on her back but she's so big she makes me small.

It may only be a fraction, a few small inches

But I could be in an aeroplane or on a mountaintop.

In my high altitude armchair, I am above my life.

I am safer here than a baby in the womb.

My big, big horse that I raised and trained becomes my guardian

And she's so big, she makes cancer small.

November 2009

Megan was not afraid of death. She knew that her spirit would live on. One day, about two months before she died, when we were alone together and she was lying in bed, not speaking because she was almost too weak to speak, just being together, she broke the silence to say in her calm but firm and matter of fact way: 'I am dying Mummy.' There was a silence. I did not speak. 'But I will never leave you.' No more was said. Those words live with me continuously. Megan was telling me that though her body might die, her spirit would live on. She would never leave me. She has not left me. This I believe.

But it is hard. What does happen when you die, Megan? I know that at that moment when you ceased to breathe, as I heard your last breath, I was aware of something … something almost visible, as though I actually saw your spirit leaving your body. And although, at that point, I had not yet begun to think on these things, I felt a compulsion to speak; to say 'May God receive your soul'. These words came from somewhere other than the self I know.

But where is that soul now, Megan? Do you hear me as I speak and write these words? Do you see me as the tears pour from my eyes? Do you feel the pain of my grief? Megan. Are you there?

Megan was a spiritual person. She believed in God and in the life of the soul after death. Her faith was very personal to her. She did not talk about it and most of those who knew her were not aware of this side of her personality. She did not demonstrate her faith by attending church services. Her spiritual beliefs were formed, beginning at a very early age, from her own experiences and her own thoughts. Her Welsh grandfather was a devout Christian, a lay reader in the Church of England. From about the age of 12, Megan used to have long phone conversations with him. There was no subject they did not discuss, including the question of the existence of God.

She explained a little of her spiritual journey in a letter to me from Edinburgh University when she was 21 years old. 'I wrote to Grampy [her grandfather] to tell him I found God! A nice Easter present for him. I think the fate of my immortal soul bothers him a lot, but no great revelation, simply a different way of looking at the same view.'

Megan's poetry is suffused with an awareness of the spirit but she rarely expressed it explicitly. In this poem, however, she does so. Written about a year before the onset of her illness, she refers to her love of horseriding and the countryside and her vocation as a veterinary surgeon.

A CURATOR OF ANGELS

Some people build cathedrals
Great towers of stone, reaching out to Heaven
And when they sing in praise or prayer
Their notes drift and float on sanctified air.

I used to climb up onto the roof
And look into the sky
For when my feet were off the ground
I could see life in sharper focus and with a wiser eye.

And I have ridden on some mighty shoulders
And felt them lift me to something close to grace
And stood beside the ocean
And sought understanding on a wide blue horizon.

But the Angel sent to watch me
Did not come from the sky or rise out of the sea.
My Angel spoke to me in the fields and on the hillside.
And it is on these green pastures beside these still waters
In delivering safely to their eternity the souls that are mine to protect,

Here is my faith, here is my mission,
Here I find God.

13 April 2008

Megan moved to Kent in 2001 to start her first job as a vet with a practice in the small market town of Faversham. It was what is known as a mixed practice, treating both horses and small animals, primarily dogs and cats. Most young vets begin their professional lives working with small animals. What drew Megan to this particular job was that it had an equine aspect to it. Her ambition at that time was to gain experience for a year or so and then return to Edinburgh to do postgraduate research with the ultimate goal of becoming an equine surgeon.

But a few months after moving to Faversham, Megan met and fell in love with a young man called Toby. Through this meeting she also developed a love of the Kentish countryside. Toby had been born and brought up in rural Kent. He was a man very much in touch with his roots. Megan and Toby shared a love of the land. Together they were in touch with the elements.

Kent is a hidden gem of a county, missed by the majority of those who pass through it on the way to the Channel ports. Despite its proximity to London and the large conurbations around the Thames Estuary, it is a surprisingly rural county. It is steeped in the history of England and crisscrossed by a multitude of tiny lanes which meander around the Downs and the ancient woods. In the Spring, these woods are carpeted by bluebells.

This poem, written a few months before the symptoms of cancer began to be felt, celebrates Megan's rapport with the spirit of the Kentish countryside.

APRIL BLUEBELL

A grey day
In a wet wood.
Smell of damp earth
And an east wind.
Could be winter still
But for a sharp green
That speaks of a warmer breeze.
But for a blue haze
Moves like mist on the marsh.
Could be the spirit of the forest.
A ghost army
Bearing aloft a memory of spring sun.
That was yesterday
With summer still to come.

27 April 2009

A year or so after starting her first job in Kent, Megan decided to set up her own equine veterinary clinic. Impatient as ever, she was not prepared to tread the traditional professional path, slowly acquiring experience, eventually perhaps becoming a partner in a practice. One of her professors at Edinburgh University told me that, despite the fact that these days it is very unusual for a young veterinarian to set up in practice on their own, he was not surprised that Megan had done so. More than 1,500 students have passed through Professor Paddy Dixon's hands since Megan was a student. Nevertheless, he remembers her well as a young woman who stood out because of her knowledge of horses, and her hard work for the vet school's herd of Exmoor ponies. She was also a memorable character. As one fellow student told me: 'In first year we were all quite quiet and shy, trying to fit in and blend in with the crowd. Not Megan! In her skin tight Levi jeans, red Welsh rugby shirt and killer high heels she marched through the echoing corridors of the "Dick Vet". You could hear it was Megan coming long before she flew round the corner and knocked you off your feet!'

The first years as a lone practitioner were hard. In order to provide a steady income, Megan took on additional weekend work as a locum at a practice which provided emergency cover for small animals, mostly dogs and cats. This is difficult work. Not for Megan the routine of inoculations and chronic diseases. Almost every animal that is brought into an emergency weekend clinic is desperately ill, either because of a worsening disease or because they have been involved in an accident. A high percentage of these cases do not survive.

Vets and doctors do very similar work. Their patients suffer from similar diseases, are victims of similar accidents. But there is one major difference, over and above the fact that a vet's patients cannot speak. In a veterinary clinic, euthanasia is common practice. Working in an emergency clinic, Megan was faced on a regular basis with making the decision as to whether her patient should die, and then of actually carrying that decision out. Once, when giving a careers talk, Megan was asked if vets got used to ending the lives of their patients. Megan's answer was no, and if they ever did they should not be in the veterinary profession.

Megan's work at the emergency clinic was physically and mentally exacting. For her, every life counted. If the suffering that an animal was enduring could not be eased, then she would take the decision to end its life. But each such decision took its toll on her. The following poem was written at that time.

GUSTAV'S VENUS

I wonder if, when I made my choices, I knew
How grave would be my dominion,
How many times each week, each day, some days each hour
I would hold a life in my hands, to be restored – or not,
That I would be a messenger of death.
And had I known that, would anything at all have changed.

I wonder what made me such a one
Who would lead so many to that dark place,
With whose heart those final beats would resonate,
By whose hand so many last breaths would drift away.
And if I could somehow hold that air in the room
Would the life remain there too.

I am she who maketh them to lie down in green pastures.
I am she who walks beside each one into the shadows.
I am she who pays the ferryman with a portion of my soul to ease their passing.
I am, each week, each day, some days each hour
An instrument of death.

We are few, the privileged ones for whom this is our calling.
Fewer still who know the weight of each life's end.
I wonder, had I known this, would my choices
Have been the same and am I glad
That I can be for some amongst my fellows
A bringer of peace.

November 2006

Megan's dedication to her job as a vet was total. The veterinary profession, said one of her colleagues, has lost an exemplary colleague. During her second year at university, she told me in a letter how she saw her future professional life.

About me: I'm not going to be the kind of vet who goes into morning surgery, does a few visits, evening surgery then goes home in the evening. I'm not even going to be like Ian Wright [a leading equine surgeon] who turns up at 6.00 am on Christmas Day to look at his patients and flies off round the world at a moment's notice to do an operation. Because I'm going to be a psychiatrist. But I'm not going to be the kind of psychiatrist who keeps a professional distance from her patients and leaves their problems in the consulting room at the end of the day. Because I'm going to be a VETERINARY psychiatrist. Animals can't remember how they felt one day to sort it out in a session the next. To fix a psychiatric problem you have to be on the spot as it happens. It's like if a composer was in a crowded restaurant and suddenly heard a tune in his head, he'd have to start singing it regardless of all the funny looks. Mine is going to be a 24 hr, 7 day, 52 weeks job and I'll probably die young (joke) – and I'm not going to take it that seriously because it's part of the job, I'm going to do the job because I want that life.

Vet. med. is my excuse to live and breathe horses for ever. It's what I do. I can't explain it any better than that so if you don't get it now you never will – which I don't mind so long as you let me get on with it. To get inside the head of a disturbed or sick horse you have to let it inside yours (like 'silence of the lambs' but more dangerous). You have to make the horse believe that you love it with absolutely everything you have – and they know when you're holding something back – and that you entrust your life to them – which you do because a pissed-off horse can easily kill a person. And you wouldn't think anyone could have enough emotional energy to keep doing that day in day out without ever getting hardened to it but what a horse will give you back is proportional to what you put in and even the smallest indicator of improvement is the most wonderful feeling on earth.

What I feel with horses surpasses not only everything else I ever felt but everything I ever heard or read or saw anyone else feel. ... When I am not with horses my heart is merely a machine that sustains the cells of my body – I am physiologically alive but I may as well be dead. When I'm riding I don't even feel good, I just am. I sing without realising.

(Extract from Megan's letter to me, May 1998)

WHATEVER

Whatever it is that I'm doing,
I wish I could stop.
Whatever it is that I'm thinking,
I wish I could stop.
And whatever it is that you want from me,
I wish I knew.
Look at the screen and concentrate.

Whatever this static time dictates,
I have no choice.
Whatever this static time thinks,
I must feel it.
But whatever it is that you want from me,
I just don't know.
Time stands still behind the glass.

However the creature breathes,
I'll be the air.
Whatever the creature needs,
I will provide.
And whatever it is that you want from me,
I wish I knew
To endeavour.

14 November 1994

Megan and Faith, 2008

PHYSICIAN OF OLYMPUS

He is not my General, nor my King.
Neither my lover nor my God.
Sometimes he is suffering, sometimes glory.
Some would have him bound, some a legend
If he had need of wings.
He has not the heart of a lion,
Yet his blood runs over the fields of war.
He has dragged our dreams through history
And carried the wind of fortune.
One day a nation's idol,
Another, worthless flesh.
To some the face of love, to some a child,
He is everything we wish for but without vice.
He is our graven image and the potter's wheel,
Though, as he walks the earth, we do not kneel.
Yet still he is not humbled, his eye is proud.
With all that he accepts, he is unbowed.
His truth and substance, I would claim my worth
In the breath of the monarch I am privileged to serve.

1 February 1999

Megan was born into a non-horsey family and yet it was obvious from about the age of three that horses were her great love. Her first riding experience was on a donkey at Weston-super-Mare when she was about 18 months old. She was captivated by it. At the age of four, I gave in to her entreaties and she began lessons at a local riding school. Throughout her life she wished that I could share her love of horses. I tried, but it was foreign territory. As part of her attempt to help me understand she sent me a lengthy essay from Edinburgh University about man's relationship with horses. It was entitled: This is a Miracle.

... Our relationships are no less valuable to us than those of the horseless. It isn't that we have no children to love. It isn't that we are in some way repressed and can express ourselves only to dumb animals. It isn't that we distrust our fellow man or are emotionally scarred to the point that we deny our humanity to identify with horses instead in the belief that they will not hurt us.

Even the horse that loves you can disappoint, betray, desert and even kill you. Violence is not alien to them – nor the desire to destroy. We don't need to find a purpose for ourselves in something utterly dependent on us. Horses are not something we retreat to when life is hard nor hide behind from the rest of the world. It isn't something we imagine in order to justify our obsession. The love of a horse is real, tangible. Anyone with eyes can see it. It is genuine and unconditional and can never be reproduced. It is without artifice or even thought.

A horse makes a man a god. They don't love us because we are beautiful or clever or funny or kind. They make no distinction between rich and poor, skilled and ham-fisted, black and white, male and female. They do not embrace the concepts of commitment and freedom and insecurity and denial. They love us or they don't. They do not justify, reason or moralise and, although they may argue with us, refuse us, leave us or even injure us, their love is simply a reflection of ours for them. And they will reward our love with performances of breathtaking energy, courage and inspiration.

They take on our characters, absorb our moods, become part of us. They are our other half. They know what we're thinking before we do. They are our vice and our conscience. They substitute nothing for there is nothing missing from our lives that we have not denied ourselves to keep them. It isn't that we are not whole or that there is something wrong with us. We have found what you all are seeking in a place you never thought to look. We are no different to you but that we know something you don't. We have the love of our horses – they are our religion, our star, our course. The only thing on earth that God created perfect.

(Extract from Megan's letter to me, August 1997)

When Megan went to university she was eligible for a small amount of grant aid. In the winter of her third year, she spent most of her scarce resources on buying an Exmoor pony. Mac was no ordinary Exmoor. He was a ten-year-old breeding stallion, never ridden, never even broken, who had come to the end of his siring days. Mac was wild and woolly and Megan loved him dearly.

The Exmoor pony is Britain's oldest breed of native pony and is an endangered species. They are herd animals, for the most part roaming freely over Exmoor and other wild parts of the country. One of the few herds outside Exmoor is owned by Edinburgh University vet school. The ponies live for the most part on the nearby Pentland Hills and are managed by vet students. During the summer they are used for pony trekking holidays.

Megan became a member of the Royal Dick Vet Exmoor Pony Society early in her student days and in 2000 became its President. She maintained her links with the society after graduating and in 2009, the year of her illness, provided a retirement home at her yard in Kent for one of the Edinburgh ponies called Eeyore. He joined Mac, who had followed Megan to Kent by way of our home in Cambridge, and two Exmoor mares from which Megan was planning to breed.

Megan and the Exmoor herd on the Pentland Hills near Edinburgh, 1998

MOTION OF THE FORWARD VARIETY

Walk beside me.
Neither pull ahead
Nor hang back
And do not follow me
But know where I go
And walk beside me there.

Walk beside me.
Stand when I stop
And walk when I go.
Step lightly over the fresh turf
Like angels dancing beneath your feet
And walk heavenly beside me.

Walk beside me
When the grass is green
And the sky is blue.
Dance like silver light
And be filled with joy
And walk beside me.

29 May 1994

Megan saw things with a different eye. She saw the natural world around her both with the freshness of a child and with the keen observation of a scientist. She had the ability to mould her words to express this wonder, this empathy with God's creatures and God's earth, this sense of the spiritual. In the doing so, she herself created a thing of beauty.

OVER THE RESIDUAL LOW

Beside the satin ice-sheen
There stands a tree, stripped bare,
Whose leaves are scattered at the base of the hill,
Whose arms reach out to the frozen sky.
And a mistle thrush stands on one frail grey branch
As he waits for the wind to change.
Then he beats of his wings, turns his head to the sun
And flies over the shimmering snow.

Beside the velvet sand-spread
A cliff looks out to sea,
Whose face is whipped by the West Wind,
Whose features are crumbled and grim.
And a gull clings to a safe stony edge
As he waits for the tide to turn.
Then he falls from the rock, soars up into the cloud
And flies over the silver-grey foam.

Beside the green of the meadow
A barn watches over his herd,
Who looks out through his spiders-web windows,
Who speaks through the cracks in his door.
And I sit on the roof of the stable
As I wait for my life to return.
Then I rise from my grief, though I'll never forget,
And fly over the residual low.

2 December 1994

Who then is this child to whom I gave birth? Who is this girl and young woman who writes so often of pain and death, of God and soul, of eternity and infinity? Who is she?

She is the same person who loved life passionately, who lived with such intensity, such joy, truly as though there were no tomorrow.

Megan was a remarkable child but I was slow to realise that. I knew little of babies and young children when she was born and so I took her abilities for granted. She was able to talk at a very early age. By the age of two we held normal conversations. A doctor at the routine check for two-year-olds asked me how many words Megan could put together. The question puzzled me. I had never counted. It was like asking me how many words the doctor could put together. Since Megan remained stubbornly mute throughout the appointment, I doubt that he believed my answer.

She was really a companion. Someone I could talk to and who would talk to me. Someone I would enjoy going for a walk with. She was always so interested in everything, fascinated by the world around her.

Megan was 16 when she wrote the following poem. I remember her showing it to me as I stood in her room one sunny day in Cambridge. I did not understand it then and I do not understand it now. But I love it.

COCO'S NEEDLES

I said to Coco in her chair,
"Why do you sit here?"
She sits in her chair with blackness ahead,
With a sound in her head and black all around,
And only her needles to sing her to sleep,
To sing her to sleep in her red chair.

I said to Coco in her chair,
"How do you weave so?"
She sits in her chair with her yarn in her hand,
With candles burnt out and yarn in her hand,
And only her mind to see the thread fly,
And sing her to sleep in her red chair.

I said to Coco in her chair,
"Who gave you your needles?"
She sits in her chair with her laugh in the air,
With a sound she can't hear and a laugh in the air,
And remembers a girl she knew ten years ago
Who'd sing to herself in that red chair.

She remembers a dress and a chain round her neck,
And red wine and candles with real flames she'd seen,
And a smile on her lips and a hand in her hand,
For he sang her to sleep in her red chair.

She remembers no tears nor promises spent,
No token of love in her desk drawer,
No bright summer's day, but a November night
When he sang her to sleep in her red chair.

I said to Coco in her chair,
"What else do you know?"
She sits in her chair not hearing my words,
With blackness around and not hearing me,
And she faces me with her back turned
As she sings to herself in her red chair.

And looks into the dark where the candles burnt out,
Says, "I can't see the lights and I can't hear the songs,
But when lovers remain just a handful of dust,
I'll still have my needles to sing me to sleep."

I said to Coco in her chair,
"Why do you sit here?"
She sits in her chair with a sound in her head,
With a story to tell and a sound in her head,
And only her needles to sing her to sleep,
To sing her to sleep in her red chair.

March 1994

When Megan was seven years old, I left her and her sister at home with their father for about a week and flew to the city of Dresden, at that time in communist East Germany behind the Iron Curtain. It was the first time I had left my children. I was revisiting a city I knew well and which meant a great deal to me. As an 18-year-old I had taken part in a project of international reconciliation there by helping to rebuild a hospital that had been largely destroyed during the Second World War bombing raid on the city. This time, in 1985, I was returning along with a number of other British people to commemorate the 40th anniversary of that raid.

This war-time anniversary was seen in Britain as a major news story. The raid had created a firestorm causing huge loss of life and massive destruction. Because of this, and coming as it did just a few months before the end of the war, the raid had continued to arouse controversy. There were television programmes about Dresden which Megan followed with great interest. I had told her about my involvement with the city and the reason why I was now going there. When I returned, my husband told me that Megan had been very disturbed by the things she had seen on the television and had wept greatly. During the next few days, she wrote a poem about Dresden.

Opposite: *Dresden after the bombing raid of February 1945*

DRESDEN COMMEMORATION

Bombing of Dresden, towering above,
Bombing of Dresden, towering above.
Bombed the mortal people,
Shattered the steeple.

Dresden a city,
Then was a ruin,
People were scattering,
Fire storm appeared.

Ruin and wreckage,
Now are moved,
Dresden a city,
Almost restored.

February 1985

Ten years later, together with others, I organised a commemorative concert in Cambridge. Megan, playing her cello, was a member of the orchestra. On the day of that concert, she wrote her second poem about Dresden.

ANNIHILA

Devastation after devastation.
To be annihilated, conflagrated, liberated.
And then be still the wind that fans the flames.
Drop to lift the dust over the stones.
Powder ash, dust of their bones.
Annihilate this place called home.

Remember, then, in their shadow
If they are watching. Stars amongst the stars,
Singing to the rooftops lest they burn away.
Libera me. Blessed they.
Tears for the requiem.
Devastation after devastation.

14 February 1995

Megan, aged two, with her father David

When Megan was 12, her father died from cancer after a short illness. Megan reacted strongly to her father's death. The hospital rang early one morning to tell me he had died. We had not been expecting the news. I prepared to go to the hospital with my two children but Megan refused. She would go to school as normal, she said, and left. I rang the school to tell them what had happened and they said they would look after her. I then left for the hospital with my younger daughter Morag, then aged ten. Megan did not cry over her father's death. On the day of the funeral she dressed herself in her brightest party clothes and smeared her lips with lipstick. As the years went by she felt a great anger over his death, an anger which was only assuaged after she met Toby and planned her own wedding. It was at this point that she began her reconciliation with her father and she spoke movingly about him at her wedding reception where his absence was so keenly felt. This reconciliation grew stronger with the birth of her own child so that by the time of Morag's wedding, just a few months before her own illness became apparent, she was able to tell Morag that she had felt her father's presence during the church service.

Megan wrote the next poem when she was 13 years old, 18 months after her father's death.

SEEING INFINITY

See this blade, so pristine sharp and shining
Point, blood red with blood that's not yet spilt.
In mirrors of its surface look that you may see infinity.
And are you frightened?

Then place the lethal weapon down
Upon the table. Free your hand.
And are you still frightened?

***

Feel the cold black metal here tightly clasped within your trembling hand.
Its end hard pressed against your head, a tunnel of ultimate death.
Through which you can see infinity.
And are you frightened?

Then, like flags unfurled, release your fingers.
Place black metal in its rack.
And are you still frightened?

***

Taste the bitter poison on your lips not yet exposed.
Sweet liqueur of your life gone past that is no longer.
One drop is all, for this wine waits for no man's strength.
And in the bottle you can see infinity.
And are you frightened?

Then take the vial and hear it fall,
Now smashéd lies on frozen ground of concrete floor.
And are you still frightened?

***

Feel now the winter's icy blast surround
Which carries you to winter's river bank.
Hear now the evil voices chant within your brain.
See now the rushing water pass your feet so gleaming clear.
Know now that this is what you fear.
And are you frightened?
Then so be it, for soon you will see infinity.

19 November 1991

'I don't believe in romantic love...' Megan told me in a letter in November 1996.

On 4 September 2004, she married Toby Broad in the ancient parish church in the village of Herne in Kent. It was a simple and beautiful ceremony. Megan had found her man. Having for most of her life sworn that she would never marry and more recently compromised by saying she could only marry another vet, Megan surprised everyone by marrying a man who was not a vet and did not ride.

Megan and Toby loved each other. During her illness he cared for her as only someone with the deepest love could do, and she, so independent, so strong, entrusted herself and her body to him.

Opposite: *Megan on her wedding day*

Megan and Toby

LUNAR SPECULATION

Where there is a crowd
There are familiar strangers
Acquaintances, smothered by their own ambiguity.
Anything they say can still wash over me.
The abyss, the sea and suddenly
A flight to plains of green.

For you are the light in the darkness of my lonely heart.
A ray from the moon, like a spotlight, picking me out from the crowd.
There is a picture and there is sunshine
And you and I are captured in the moment's light.
A lunar solstice, to look once is to be forever.

And there I can say I love you
And always know you understand.
Asking questions of a concept is not a part of the heartland
And for you, I am the overriding instinct.
I calm your fear and you will always love me.

For as long as love will overcome darkness
In your eyes I am love itself
And for me you are the only truth.

20 August 1993

Megan and Amos, aged two days

Amos was born at home on 19 January 2008. Megan was totally opposed to the idea that birth was a medical procedure and adamant that her baby would be born at home. She had been present at numerous animal births and saw the arrival of new life as a totally natural event. Amos was delivered by an independent midwife called Virginia. She and Megan were two of a kind. Strong women. They understood each other. When Virginia asked Megan what she wanted from her midwifery care, Megan said that she had no intention of getting on a 'conveyer belt of care' and told Virginia: 'I want to be in charge! My body, my pregnancy, my labour, my baby. I want to feel I have the best information available in order to form my own judgements and make my own decisions about my care and that those choices will be supported. I do not want my needs subjected to someone else's perceived notion of what is best for the baby.'

At Megan's funeral, Virginia quoted these words in a tribute she paid to a woman she admired. Megan had told Virginia that the birth was going to be like a party. Virginia noted down exactly what Megan told her. She remembered thinking that it could all change on the actual day of the birth because birth can be tough, but in the event, she said, it really was like a party. 'No drama, no fuss and on a cold January day just two short years ago Megan birthed a beautiful, healthy, strong Amos at home on the farm she loved with the husband she loved, exactly like she had predicted and just like the strong confident woman I knew.'

Megan died, at home, a few hours before Amos' second birthday. There had been talk the week before her death of celebrating the birthday in the Pilgrims Hospice in Canterbury where she was then being cared for. But as her condition worsened, the decision was made to bring her home. I sat with her as she died and watched her bring her own life to a close. I believe she managed her death, and chose to die the day before Amos' birthday not wishing to leave him with the legacy of her death and his birth being marked on the same date.

THE REST OF FOREVER

Remember, little children I will never know,
Your precious lives.
Your vision, your truth.
Go forward, little children of the sterile seed
And walk towards your home.

A poison in your blood, each hour of night,
Would clip your wings
But 'let me fly' your prayer.
For waiting for your virtue makes you beautiful.
What price your home?

Forgive her, little children who are not my own.
Her die is cast,
Her future her own dream.
She rises, little children, she will live again
From exile, home.

And she is not Jerusalem, my children.
She is the sea,
The air of the abyss
And all she asked was life, my little children,
To bring her angel home.

Forever, little children, is eternity
Unwavering,
Horizon in the sky.
So dedicate your souls, my never children,
To watch the sunrise.

The choice you make, your purpose, is your legacy
Your pride
Your righteousness
And mine, my single-handed wish will be my judgement
And let me breathe.

13 June 1999

We will always be the three Ms, Morag told Megan as she sat at her bedside the morning of the day she died. Merrilyn, Megan and Morag. The three Ms. That is how we were known, especially after the death of my husband, united yet more closely by our common loss.

The bond between the two sisters was always strong. 'My sister' is how Megan thought of Morag with the emphasis on the 'my'. She loved her little sister from the start with no hint of jealousy. The two girls were not alike but there was a strong emotional bond between them, a childhood closeness that grew as their personalities developed in different ways in their teenage years. Both were strong characters, Morag quietly so. Both would defend the other to the last.

It was not easy being Megan's sister. Megan – older, taller, louder, cleverer. The teachers at school often muddled the names, calling Morag by her sister's name, but never the other way round.

Shortly after Megan's death, a schoolfriend of Morag who had known both girls wrote to Morag: 'Our sisters are our allies – more so than our mothers and our husbands. When we were young our lives were completely intertwined. We give them nieces and nephews who sense our special relationship and who love them. We expect to share our lives with them as we grow old and that they will endure alongside us when our parents and husbands are gone. We expect our children to cherish them in their old age. I feel so sad that you have lost Megan.'

At the time of Megan's death, Morag was living in Paris with her French husband Nicolas. She never returned to her French home, remaining in Kent to help Toby care for two-year-old Amos as Megan had wished and as Morag had promised to do. Nicolas joined her three months later and two months after that their son Hugo was born.

Megan, Merrilyn and Morag

Megan and Morag preparing for Morag's wedding, 2009

APOLOGIES I

In the beginning there was you and me,
And what was mine was mine was mine
And what was yours was yours was yours
And it was good.

Then you and I were joined in age,
And what was mine was mine was mine
And what was yours was yours and mine
And I liked it so.

I called it sharing. I liked it so.
You were quiet. I liked it so.
And I was there and you were there
And now you're not.

Then what was yours was yours and yours
And what was mine was mine and mine
And freedom to be mine was mine
But I missed you.

Perhaps there was too much of me.
Too much was mine and mine and mine
But I like me and mine and mine.
But I love you.

Sometime past [probably around 1992]

Megan described herself as a wordsmith. She was a huge respecter of language, could not bear to see words misused.

In a letter to me from university one day, apropos of nothing in particular, she wrote: '... You may have noticed the recent burgeoning of my passion for words – I think they are a miraculous thing (Gielgudism!) – in my book [she was writing a novel at the time], in conversation, in all things I would like to be able to create not just pictures but evocations, sensations with words. I think it is utterly deplorable that people are too stupid and lazy to use the enormous wealth of words available to express themselves... '

One day during her illness, when she was in hospital, I took in with me the draft of a talk I was due to give on the Cold War as part of my work as a historian. I had thought I might work on it while she slept. But she encouraged me to read it to her, which I did. She then critiqued it, both for its content and its writing. I was amazed that after one reading she was able to hold this talk in her head in such detail, so much so that she was able to pick up on small points of grammar. Next time I write a book, I will ask you to edit it, I said. Yes, she said. Do that.

During the many days that Megan spent in hospital during her illness, she passed some of the time doing the crosswords I brought in for her. She had a phenomenal memory and a mental data bank of general knowledge that astounded us, her family. Where had it come from, we often wondered as Megan once again came out victorious in Christmas quizzes. She did her last crossword five days before she died. We were alone together in the hospital and we worked on it while waiting for test results. Megan was feeling unwell but was coping. Then she said, with a worried look, that she was finding it difficult to hold anagrams in her head. I tried to soothe her. I could never do that at the best of times, I told her. Later, I realised that that moment was the beginning of the end. It was the moment when Megan realised that her amazing mind, the thing that was central to her being, was failing her.

AWAKENING

Sleep until the world awakens you.
I am your strength.
Sleep until the stars awaken you.
I am your success.
Spin until the earth awakens you.
I am your weakness.
Spin until the water awakens you.
I am your death.

I am the powerless God.
I am the frail leader.
I am the conquering victim.
I am the feeble martyr.
I am the foolish liar.
I am the solo partner.
I am the helpless winner.
I am the crushed hero.

Consider this a great achievement.
To waste a life this well.
Spin until the water awakens you.
I am your death.
Consider this my last great gesture.
Like a star exploding.
Spin until the water awakens you.
I am your death.

Consider this my Matin Perpetual.
This is my end.

June 1994

Megan was also a musician. Not a star pupil or the one singled out for glory at the school concert but a lover of music who played the piano and the cello and, most importantly, composed her own music. She was never content to play other people's music. Even as a small child she reckoned that she could improve on anything Mozart wrote – and did so to the surprise of her piano teacher. When she was seven, she composed and played the background music for a book launch at her school. She was invited to do this by one of the other parents, the children's author and illustrator Gillian McClure, whose book *Tog the Ribber*, later short-listed for the Smarties Award, was about to be published.

'Megan was the most exceptional and unusual child I think I have ever known,' Gillian told Megan's family and friends at her funeral. Recalling the launch of *Tog the Ribber*, she described how the children at school made shadow puppets and put on a magical show. 'But it was the music – haunting and original – that held everything together – and that was composed by seven-year-old Megan.'

Megan is obviously something rather precious, musically speaking, another of her music teachers told me when Megan was a teenager. Around this time Megan composed a piece for piano and saxophone called *Indelible Expression* and performed it, together with her sister Morag on saxophone, at a school concert. She transposed the final two lines of this poem as the sub-heading to the composition. It is one of many pieces she composed.

SPRECHENSANG

If music be the food of love
Play on for me, my love.
If music be a way of life
I live for you, my love.
To sign my name in sprechensang
Where noble kings and princes leap.
Expressions only words and notes
Where others stumble I will keep.
For music be my alibi
And sure, you let her in, not I.
But, beneath music as my guise
Your soul is mine my love.
Thus, I will tame the spirit so,
Play on for us to dance and lo
Beneath the moon, with music soft
Our hearts combine and harmonise.
Forever and always indelible on my mind
As music might fade but never is lost.

December 1992

Indelible Expression

"As music might fade but never is lost,
forever and always, indelible on my mind"

andante espressivo e cantabile

da coda al fine

And then there is the world we live in, a world of which Megan was very much a part. She helped to run the Venture Scouts and the business enterprise group at school, was elected as a student representative at university, devoured newspapers. She was not particularly interested in party politics but cared deeply about justice. This is a political poem.

ANTHEM FOR THE SAFETY NET

Do you remember the colour of rain?
That some would believe it was red?
It rained on the marchers who stormed the town hall
And they thought it was stained with their blood.
When they called to the nameless faceless
They believed they would die for their cause
But would they have run for cover
If someone had opened fire?

Do you remember the colour of iron?
That some would believe it was red?
It rained on the few who climbed over the wall
And they thought it was draped in the flag.
When they died on the barbed wire fences
They thought they had died to be free
But the thousands who watched in silence,
Ten thousand times freer were they.

Do you remember the colour of power?
That some would believe it was red?
It rained on the workers who vote with their feet
And they thought they had cut through the tape.
When they stood by the picket-line fences
They thought that they might even win
But they'll take their two percent pay rise
Because it's easier to give in.

Do you remember the colour of freedom?
That some would believe it was red?
It rained on the writers who fled from their homes
And they suffered for the printed word.
When they died, forgotten, in exile
They thought they had died with their cause
But true revolution is stronger
Than those kept behind closed doors.

February 1996

Megan was fascinated by all living creatures. As a child she collected snails and beetles. Later she bred stick insects in the kitchen. When she was 18 she found a fledgling sparrow on the pavement in Newmarket where she was working as a groom at an equine veterinary practice in order to gain work experience. The bird had fallen from its nest. She took it back to the spartan flat where she was living, above the stables, and nursed the little bird to maturity. She imitated the parent birds by dangling raw mince from tweezers above its head, thus encouraging it to eat. As it grew bigger it used to fly around the room and settle on her head or shoulder. I could hear the bird tweeting loudly down the phone when I called her, making it difficult to hold a conversation. The bird became very tame and she brought it to visit us at home in Cambridge. There, it sat happily on our dog's back. When the bird was ready to live independently, we took it to a bird and animal sanctuary near Cambridge where they kept it in partial captivity before releasing it back into the wild when it was ready and able to go.

Two months after writing the next poem, Megan left home to begin her veterinary medicine studies at Edinburgh University. 'I am about to embark on the hardest five years of my life,' she wrote.

Megan and Tweetipie, July 1996

Earlier that year, she had gone to Northumberland to work with a hill farmer during the lambing season. For vet students, lambing is an essential part of their training. This was Megan's first experience of the work. It was tough, out on the hills, very often at night, helping ewes to bring their lambs into the world in the cold and dark. It was basic and bloody. The result of one particularly difficult birth was a dead ewe and a sickly lamb with a broken leg. Megan put a splint on the leg (her first attempt at healing a fracture) and placed the lamb in the bottom of the farmhouse Aga – a makeshift incubator. The next morning the farmer told Megan that the lamb was too weak to survive. It would go the way of all such lambs. But, he added, Megan could have it if she wanted. This was Megan's final day at the farm. She took the lamb, picked up her rucksack, and got on the train back to our home in Cambridge.

The first I knew of any of this was when I went to meet Megan off the train in the afternoon. There, striding towards me down the platform came my daughter with a rucksack over one arm and an orphaned lamb under the other. Accustomed as I was to various sickly birds and animals being brought into the house, this was nevertheless a surprise. We all piled into the car, the lamb giving the occasional bleat, and set off home. It so happened that the following day Megan was due to leave home again to begin work on a pig farm some distance away. That left me and my younger daughter Morag to look after the lamb. He was christened Splinty. There began a frantic search for powdered ewes' milk and the appropriate bottle with which to feed him. Splinty was housed in the downstairs loo and Morag I and shared the frequent feeding shifts that were necessary for such a young and sickly lamb. His pathetic bleats of hunger would bring us staggering from our beds at five in the morning.

Splinty thrived and became a large strapping lamb. He was transferred to the coal shed (minus coal) and gambolled on the lawn with the dog. Megan found a new home for him as a companion for a friend's horse. The day before he was due to leave, Splinty died. It was sudden and unexpected. It is hard, I am told, to keep lambs alive. All three of us were devastated.

TIME TO FLY

Did you give me wings, little bird, to fly,
That I might leave you now, forever,
That dangers I might face head-on, alone
And challenge you before my life is done?

Did you give me heart, little bird, to love,
That I might e'er deny your brand of truth,
That life might mean a different tune to me,
Will you be disappointed when I'm done?

Did you give me eyes, little bird, to see,
That I might find my vision somewhere new,
That blind ambition take me to that place
And I would see you cry before I'm done?

Did you give me soul, little bird, and strength,
That I might chose the path for my belief,
That battles may be fought and races run?
Nay, you will see me win e're I am done.

20 July 1996

This poem was written while Megan was lambing the following year in the Scottish borders.

GOOD ENOUGH FOR ROTAS

Would that I were Alpha to your Omega.
Would that I were distance to your time.
Would that I, alone amid your company
Were granite to your lime.

Would that I were lead to hang your plumbline.
Would that I were grist to feed your mill.
Would that I were truth within your prophecy,
The force which binds your will.

Would I were a knife to twist inside you.
Would that I were salt to treat your wounds.
Would that I were sand when you were thirsty.
Folly to your fool.

The morning star, the halo of the heavens,
The dew that hangs like crystals on the vine,
The bright, the beautiful, all of His creations,
As much are mine.

10 April 1997 (1.30am!)

Megan and Splinty, April 1996

My family has been farming the land of North Pembrokeshire for generations stretching back into the mists of time. My uncle did so well into his 90s and it was on this farm that Megan felt a sense of home. Although I was not brought up in Wales, as a child I spent my summer holidays there visiting my grandfather and I followed this same tradition with my own children. That part of Pembrokeshire is steeped in paganism and early Christianity. There is a mysticism to the craggy and untamed landscape of that rugged coast that was sensed by the men who lived there in centuries past. Ancient cromlechs (prehistoric burial grounds) and stone circles litter the hills and fields. And in the little city of St David's, a great cathedral stands on the site of a monastery established by the patron saint of Wales in the sixth century.

Megan aged 18 on the North Pembrokeshire coast

When Megan was 21, she wrote to me from Edinburgh:

*'Today I had a revelation. Actually there were two but the first
was more of a peculiar vision, a flash of memory in unusual
circumstances.*

*You know how some days ('There is a time on certain days/As
evening draws to night, they say') – nothing to do with what I'm
about to describe but the phrasing reminded me of that.*

*Anyway, in Pembrokeshire, sometimes the sky goes a sort of smoky
violet colour in the early afternoon when it is very hot indeed and
you feel everyone should be asleep under a tree and they probably
are because there never seems to be anyone about. And there is a
film of brown dust on everything and a dusty 'freezing fog' effect
about 18 inches off the ground. And you can't see the sun although
there are no clouds, only the general direction of the light. And the
air smells faintly of the sea and wheat husks from Uncle Ewan's
grain store and a little of egg sandwiches.*

*Well, for just a few seconds, today I could smell that smell – in
Midlothian, through the car window. It was very odd – I haven't
smelt it for years and it took me home...'*

21 October 1998

Megan's Rock in its raw state on the Pembrokeshire hillside

WHERE CARREG WAS

(Carreg means 'stone' in Welsh)

Once, where Carreg was, I sank into the earth
And there my strength was found anew
And there I heard the bells announce my coming
And there the rock was warm to warm my blood
And I was home where I belonged.

Once, where Carreg was, my blue-blue-green
Did breathe for me the air from the abyss,
Did land my feet on angel grass,
Did shine on me a panoramic sunlight
And I was home where I was loved.

Once, where Carreg was, it rained a day
And in a second I was lost
And all the morning I did cry more rain
And hoped to build a face for evening
When I began my long deceit.

Once, where Carreg was, I knew my home
And I was drawn there in my sleep as prayer
But I have lied to my angel
And I have stolen from the rock
Can I ever return?

before 16 November 1996

About a month before she died, Megan celebrated Christmas at my home, together with Toby, Amos, Morag and her husband Nicolas. Megan had been determined that it would be a good Christmas. Christmas mattered to her; it always had done. She had taken enormous trouble, using her limited energy, to find everyone the right presents and to send out her cards. She arrived at my home looking beautiful. The first thing she did was to sit down at the piano with Amos on her knee and play *Away in a Manger*, softly singing the words to her child. She spent much of the day sitting on the sofa, sometimes asleep, but partaking of the present opening and the eating of the traditional meal. By the evening we were all tired. But Megan seemed reluctant to leave. It was as though she did not want the day to come to an end. She never entered my house again.

Two days later her condition deteriorated and she was readmitted to hospital. From there she was eventually transferred to the Pilgrims Hospice, not because she was dying, they said, but because she could receive better care there. Megan liked it. She had a lovely room of her own and the staff were kind and thoughtful. Amos was there most days and the staff said they would hold a party for him on his second birthday. But a few days before that, very suddenly, Megan became extremely ill, so much so that she could barely speak or move. We arranged for her to come home. There was nothing more that could be done. On the evening of the third day, I sat by her bedside holding her hand and listening to her laboured breathing. Beside me sat a volunteer from the hospice.

She began to ask me about Megan. And so I told her, with pride and love, the story of Megan and her love of horses, from the beginnings on a seaside donkey to having her own pony as a child, from Mac the Exmoor to Lochan the eventer, and then on to Ochre, the big big horse, and many many more. A minute or so after I came to the end of my story, I noticed a change in Megan's breathing. It had become slower, more deliberate. We called for Toby who had been with Amos. Although the hospice volunteer told me that Megan could continue to live for a day or even two, I knew she was dying. About twenty minutes later she drew her last breath. She was entirely peaceful and entirely in control. Megan had chosen the time of her dying.

It was only later, when I thought back on it, that I realised that the change in Megan's breathing had taken place at exactly the time that I had finished relating the story of her life with horses. Megan had heard me. She had heard in my voice that this was something that mattered to me too. I had chosen to talk not about my daughter's academic abilities nor her many artistic talents, not about her successful career nor even her astonishing poetry, but about the thing that mattered to her the most throughout her life. And by doing so I had given Megan, perhaps at last, that which she had sought in life and appealed for so movingly in her introduction to her poetry – understanding, love and belief.

And so she was able to go.

PERPETUAL MORNING

Optimism, hope, I made plans for our future.
I could still see the sun through the dark clouds above.
And even when the rain came down and soaked me
I thought of the rainbow that would never come.

The pink glow in the sky that I saw as beautiful
Was reflected only in the storm clouds that blacked out the sun.
And when the new moon rose, I saw hope in its gleam
When really it was just someone's cynical joke.

Shepherds' warning should have been my warning too.
I made promises that weren't up to me to keep.
And now I am sorry for getting your hopes up.
The rains that fall are my tears from heaven.

My perpetual morning is of the other kind
Where the truth is worse than the nightmare.
The kind of grieving for what I haven't lost.
Please. Let there be light.

14 April 1994

OCEANUS

Oh happy tears,
That they might fall once more
On the baked, barren earth
And from there
A mighty flood bring forth.
Whispers on the water,
Silver bells glinting through the spray
And where her white horses
Rise to meet the sea
On an ocean-going breeze
Who can tell?
Happy tears,
Bring deliverance to me.
Happy tears,
Whose salt was once the sea.

17 January 1995 and July 2001

Wish
Dream
Believe
Breathe

*These words were inscribed on the back of a watch that
Megan gave to her husband Toby.*

*The same words have been inscribed inside the natural basin of
Megan's Rock by the sculptor Darren Yeadon.*